BECOMING HIS DESIRE

Essential keys to becoming the woman every man needs and wants to keep

SYLVIA TITUS

Contents

INTRODUCTION

Most women nowadays would say that the sort of lady men admire and can't live without is an Angelina Jolie doppelganger, or at the absolute least blond, blue-eyed, and have great legs. While this sort of lady would certainly draw a lot of attention, she isn't the type of woman these men are looking for.

That's fantastic news for the majority of us, ladies! While men are visual beings, and their first attraction is based on appearances, you'd be shocked at how much more men seek from women.

For instance, a group of sociologists performed research to see if there was a common denominator that men found beautiful in women; if there was one element that would make any male want to approach a lady and chat to her. You'd never predict what the outcome would be. It wasn't her breasts, legs, or bottom that did it. It wasn't any portion of her body below her chin, and it wasn't even her looks. It was her grin that did it. Nothing, according to the majority of men, is more appealing than a woman's grin.

The idea of this insight is that you must set aside your preconceived assumptions as well as the restrictions that society has instilled in you. You must realize that males and women are essentially different, and it is perfectly OK to be a woman. There's nothing wrong with handing over power to your spouse every now and again, especially if it makes you feel better.

In the workplace and maybe other parts of our life, society may have put men and women on an equal footing. While it is true that a woman can accomplish practically whatever a male can do, and vice versa, it is also true that we are hardwired with basic distinctions. The trouble is that when we try to ignore those differences and pretend they don't exist, we wind up sealing ourselves off from the rest of the world in order to be more like the males we feel compelled to compete with.

This is particularly common in the office, but sadly, many women extend this conduct into their personal life, and they end up harming themselves and their relationships.

Women are sometimes terrified of being women, of seeming feminine or fragile, since they associate femininity with weakness. The reverse is true since a woman who is in touch with herself and reveals her fragility has far more influence over a guy than a woman who acts tough all of the time.

In this book, we'll look at many of the distinctions between men and women, and how those differences provide us more strength than any regulations society may try to impose. You will become the girl who all men desire and can't live without once you let your inner femininity show through.

CHAPTER ONE

Being a Lady

Many of the issues we have in our relationships arise from a lack of comprehension or the fact that we don't understand why males act the way they do. Indeed, individuals frequently have no idea why they act the way they do, so it's no wonder that we have difficulty understanding their answers.

However, before we dive into these basic distinctions, it's important to take a step back and look in the mirror, because we'll never be able to make the required adjustments to become the woman men admire unless we learn to truly embrace who and what we are.

The most serious issue we face right now is our self-perception. Women's liberation has been pushed to a whole new level, and instead of merely implying that women should have equal rights to males in society, it has come to indicate that women should stop acting like women and start acting like men.

The explanation for this is straightforward. Men are naturally competitive, but women are not. As a result, in order to thrive in the job, an increasing number of women have had to become just as competitive as males, if not more so, because they begin with a disadvantage in the eyes of the competition. They're females. Unfortunately, many women have pushed this competitiveness to new heights, and their desire to succeed has convinced them that being a woman equates to being weak, so they must suppress their emotions and appears more like the males they work with.

Unfortunately, women are misled, because our femininity is not a flaw, but rather strength because it is the one thing that allows us to influence men far more successfully than any argument or competition. Because males were created to battle and women were created to nurture, men are disarmed by a woman's gentleness.

Being a woman is difficult, multidimensional, and frequently unjust. It's a gender that's tough to identify with. Society holds us to absurd standards, archaic gender conventions pervade our everyday lives, gender wage discrepancies persist, and the patriarchy, despite its detractors, remains a powerful force to be reckoned with.

Being a woman entails a wide range of responsibilities. Being a woman entails being strong and forceful while yet being kind. It entails being sensitive and vulnerable toward the people we care about without feeling weak. It entails pursuing our objectives despite whatever obstacles we may face along the road. A strong female support system that inspires us to be our best selves contributes significantly to this.

Being a woman may take many forms. Womanhood is a source of strength for some. Others are moved by tenderness. Womanhood may entail challenging yourself in school or in your work, as well as assisting others in their upward mobility. You can be a woman in a dress with heels or lacing up your work boots. Relationships, employment, bodily parts, or anything else do not define womanhood; it is determined by no one or nothing except you. Being a woman entails overcoming obstacles. It is a source of strength and power.

Being a woman entails having a strong sense of self, respecting your body as one that adapts and develops through time, being self-assured, and empowering others around you. It implies that you have the foresight to be appreciative for what you have while being eager for more. On all levels, it entails keeping an eye out for other women and young girls.

Ways to Be a Better Woman

Many women have been acknowledged across the world for their great accomplishments and unique life stories. Despite their tremendous achievements, they are just like the rest of us - human, ordinary, and just like you. Everything they've done stems from their personal desire for personal self-discovery. If you want to begin your own exciting journey, focus on becoming a better version of yourself, both as a woman and as a person, now.

Here are some tips on how to be a better lady.

1. Take care of yourself

Focusing on self-love is the first step in becoming a better woman. It's not the same as being self-centered; it's about pouring enough love into yourself to be able to share that love with others: friends, family, and perhaps a special someone.

People who really love themselves understand how to look after others because they understand how to offer and share love without asking anything in return. Selflessness makes them better ladies as well as better people.

2. Recognize your worth

If you want to improve on yourself, you must first recognize your value. If you understand your value, you'll be able to judge how others should treat you – and you'll be able to spot the indicators when others are already using or abusing you. Great women understand that they should be respected and cherished for who they are, regardless of ethnicity, socioeconomic standing, or the sorts of relationships they participate in.

3. Place a high value on your relationships

Appreciate your relationships with others, especially those with people who genuinely care about and love you for who you are. Be thankful for the folks who are constantly there in your life and appreciate them. A wise lady recognizes the value of meaningful connections. You're also reminding them that their presence counts - that they make a difference in your life – by expressing that you appreciate their efforts.

4. Allow nobody to put you down.

Other people's remarks aren't as important as your own opinions. Only you have the capacity to know how much you are up to the task of, so don't allow anyone else to tell you otherwise. Continue to follow your ambitions and believe in yourself as long as you know you are not hurting anyone.

5. Put yourself out there in all you do

You have the freedom to be yourself. Show your originality through your expressions: clothes, sense of style, culinary preferences, music preferences, and anything else that will draw attention to your personality. You live in a free society where you can be who you want to be – and if you're being oppressed or denied the things that make you feel lively, it's time to activate your inner lady warrior and strive for what you deserve.

6. Don't let stereotypes hold you back from realizing your full potential

In relation to the preceding part, you must discover your inner warrior and battle against society's repressive and frequently discriminatory perceptions about women. You are not a damsel in distress; you are not timid; you are not susceptible. In your own way, you are strong and capable. You'll be unstoppable the day you discover your full potential as a woman and as a human.

7. Recognize and appreciate your inner beauty

You are stunning on the inside and out, and it's past time you acknowledged it. It's fine if, on the other hand, you're still working on recognizing your own power and attractiveness as a woman. You may begin by looking after yourself on all levels: physically, psychologically, and emotionally. A beautiful lady understands her value, potential, and strength. A beautiful lady understands that beauty is more than simply physical appearance.

8. Be Proud Of Your Achievements

Be proud of your accomplishments no matter where you are in life or what you have accomplished. Do not compare your life to that of others. Rather, concentrate on your own personal development, not only as a woman but also as a person. Small steps, huge steps, a lengthy stride, or even a sprint - no matter how quickly or slow you go, know that you are making progress. Take pride in who you are.

9. Have the courage to be firm in your convictions

Make a strong case for your position. Even if you are a woman, you have a voice that you must protect with courage and determination.

You must understand your role and obligation in protecting the rights of your fellow women – and, of course, other people – in order to become a better woman.

Fight for what you believe in, but have an open mind as well. Being a better person and a better woman often entails being willing to accept your errors and flaws in your judgments.

10. Appreciate the fact that you are alive every single day

Take pleasure in your existence. The most authentic and honest method to become a better woman is to be grateful for your existence because you have this chance to live and make a difference. You weren't sent on this planet merely to breathe and exist; you're here for a reason, whether it's for yourself or for others. Make your presence felt.

11. Serve as an example to other women

Be an encouraging and motivating role model for other women throughout the world. Demonstrate to them what it is to be able to express yourself freely and not be scared of the obstacles that lie ahead. Demonstrate to them that they, too, can be happy, healthy, fearless, and powerful like you.

You don't have to be special to make a significant difference as a woman; as previously said, the world's most prominent female icons began as regular individuals.

CHAPTER TWO

Men and Women Have Distinctive Differences

Men and women are different not just physically but intellectually, emotionally and in every wise. These differences aren't bad in themselves but they bring out the uniqueness in both gender. These differences make us compatible and understanding these differences will bring peace and understanding between spouses, friends and siblings alike. In this chapter we will look at some important differences between men and women.

1. Women Provide Advice, While Men Provide Solutions

Many ladies don't seem to realize that guys are entirely different from women. They have various ways of processing information, relating to one another, and expressing themselves. A lady who recognizes these distinctions, on the other hand, will become a rare gem that men will admire. "Love is lovely, and it may stay if we recognize our differences.

Indeed, it is precisely these distinctions between men and women that arouse desire and love, for without them, men would not require women and vice versa.

2. Understanding Men

Yes, it is possible to comprehend men, and it is probably simpler for us to comprehend them than it is for them to comprehend us. First and foremost, you must recognize that success and accomplishment are the primary motivators for males. They place a premium on measurable outcomes, efficiency, and power, and everything they do is aimed towards demonstrating their worth.

Men prefer to participate in competitive activities where they can win rather than hang about and chat about their feelings. It allows them to demonstrate their dominance over other guys. A male will not be found reading the latest issue of People or Cosmopolitan, but rather the sports section of the newspaper or the news. He is uninterested in romance books since he is more concerned with things than with feelings. And he enjoys items that let him display his power, whether it's a flashy sports vehicle or the latest electronics.

3. Advice vs. Solutions

Men are goal-oriented, and they feel good about themselves when they achieve their objectives because it demonstrates their value and competence. It is an even bigger testimonial to their power and strength if they accomplish it on their own.

Men seldom discuss their concerns because they are predisposed to fix things on their own. When they do, it signifies they require assistance and counsel.

Women will understand why men dislike being chastised or counseled without asking for it if they understand this side of males. It makes them feel inept as if you don't trust them to tackle the situation on their own.

This is also why, when women talk to them about their issues, males are more likely to propose solutions. It's because if another guy shares his troubles, it's an unspoken plea for assistance, and he considers it an honor to help.

It is a sign of his love when he gives a solution for the lady he loves, but when a woman becomes upset because she believes he isn't listening or emphasizing, he has no idea what he did to hurt her. As a result, he withdraws and effectively shuts her out.

4. Stress Management

Men and women deal with stress in various ways. A lady will tell her friends about all of her troubles, and they will immediately sense that she needs some help and understanding, so they will sympathize. Men, on the other hand, are more likely to withdraw and focus on a different task in order to tune out their concerns until the next day, when they must deal with them. Most women mistakenly believe he doesn't care about her or is ignoring her because he doesn't talk about his difficulties with her, but it's simply a question of how men and women deal with stress. You must recognize that expecting a man to open up to you instantly when he is anxious is impractical, just as expecting a man to expect you to calm down and be sensible and logical all of the time is unrealistic. You must realize that just because he withdraws to watch football or read the newspaper doesn't mean he doesn't love you; rather, it indicates that he is really agitated. You must learn to not take it personally and to allow him some breathing room. Furthermore, you will discover that if you ask for his attention in a calm and collected manner, he will be far more attentive than if you start the blame game.

Males have an outward orientation toward life

- It is exploratory. Every youngster and man is on a mission. He discovers his true self "out there" in the world, where he believes his greater purpose and destiny reside.
- Determined to "get the job done." A guy invests a great deal of faith in his ability to fulfill the mission and complete the work at hand.
- Has a strong desire to know what will happen next. He doesn't "cuddle," "savor" significant events, or "linger" in the moment way a woman does. In general, he's eager to get started on the next project.

- Taking advantage of the situation. To put it another way, the guy is a doer, and his sentiments about what he's doing or his reasons for doing it are less significant to him than the desire and opportunity to complete the task.
- Takes risks. A boy or a man must be willing to take risks in order to grab and maximize his prospects. As a result, the male character is defined by a willingness to take calculated risks.
- Aggressive and active. The link between initiating and actual aggressiveness is evident. In light of this, it's worth noting that the male brain has a core dedicated to aggressiveness and action that is two-and-a-half times bigger and more important than the female brain.
- Dominant and competitive. Men crave the greatest and will go to great lengths to have it.
- Initiator All of this presupposes a willingness and capacity to "grab the bull

by the horns" and get things done. It also implies that, while leadership is not always a male-only trait, it is more firmly established in the character of men and boys.

A woman's point of view is more internally focused

- "Confidently attractive." Unlike the guy, who has to go out into the world to find his destiny, the female has her own destiny. She has a quiet but strong belief in it.
- Prioritizes closeness over action. A woman is more concerned with being than with doing, and she discovers the cause for her existence in a relationship.
- Selectively (wisely) receptive. A woman does not get into relationships haphazardly, despite the fact that she values them beyond all else. She takes her time making decisions and receiving gifts.

- Seeks safety. The female of the species prioritizes protection and security because her orientation is inward, toward connections, caring, and "nesting." She appreciates attributes like "dependability" and "trustworthiness" in a possible spouse significantly more than the male.
- Is a humble person. A self-assured woman recognizes that she owns something really important – the power of her femininity – and is motivated by an instinctual desire to safeguard it. Her modesty is ingrained in her personality.
- Compassion. Females are more naturally motivated to respond with compassion and care to worried, needy, or hurting people.
- Makes use of language. Men converse to exchange information or ideas. Women converse to express their ideas and thoughts. As a result, women are

more likely than males to utilize more words.

- Wants to be treated fairly and submit to authority. A woman aspires to be a man's equal, but a very particular type of equal. She has a burning urge to be directed, protected, and cared for on a deep and fundamental level.
- Uses "soft power" to influence humanity. In marriage and domestic relationships, women have the power to exert both direct and indirect influence.
- Creating a connection. Females are hardwired to interact with others in a variety of ways.

CHAPTER THREE

The Influence of a Woman

When we feel our partners are ignoring us, we appear to believe that the best approach to influence them is to nag, scold, or shut down. The problem is that we expect guys to read our minds and comprehend what we want from them most of the time. Unfortunately, for the sheer fact that men process feelings and emotions in such different ways, this is the road that will lead to the destruction of any relationship. A woman, for example, prefers to talk about her difficulties, whereas males are more introverted and prefer to solve their problems on their own. When a male confides in someone about his issues, he is typically seeking advice or a solution, which is why when women disclose their concerns; they are more likely to provide solutions. The problem is that when we express our problems, we typically don't want to hear a solution; all we want is to be heard, understood, and held accountable. Someone who can sympathize with us is what we're looking for. Men, on the other hand, don't know how to empathize since it's not in their DNA. When males talk to one other about their issues, it's an indication that they're looking for help, since they're not asking for an understanding "Hmmm" and a hug, which is what we women anticipate. So, therefore, when he begins to suggest a solution, we become enraged that he doesn't comprehend what we want, despite the fact that he just doesn't know.

Women, on the other hand, have a potent "weapon," if you can call it that, to influence males. It's rooted in our frailty. The effects of opening your heart and sharing your actual sentiments will astound you. Allowing yourself to be vulnerable does not imply that you are weak. It just means that you are strong enough to embrace the possibility of being harmed if you open yourself up. Indeed, by allowing yourself to be vulnerable and express a complete range of feelings, you will be better equipped to look after yourself since you will be able to tell him exactly what you want and need. There are few things that make a guy happier than knowing that he can make his girlfriend happy, and when she is unhappy, he wants to do everything he can to make her feel better. You will discover that if you can learn to honestly convey your thoughts to him rather than reciting a laundry list of complaints, he will become a lot more receptive.

Ways a Woman Influences a Man

1. Men find it simpler to run in the presence of women

According to a new study, males find it simpler to run when ladies are present. When a male saw the final half, a woman watched the last half, and no one watched the last half, ten men were asked to assess the difficulty of 20-minute runs. The findings showed that when runners knew a woman was looking, they reported lower perceived effort than when no one was watching; when they knew a guy was watching, they reported higher perceived effort than when no one was watching. (The impact of canine observers was not investigated.)

2. Men take more risks when there are ladies around

Several studies have found that when women are around, males engage in riskier conduct. Men came to catch a 9:40 a.m. bus later than women, who arrived at the relatively safe hour of 9:35 a.m., according to research from the University of Liverpool. Men were also more likely to cross a street when automobiles were going by when women were present, "as if this was their way of showing off for the other sex," according to the researchers. (Hot!) Similar results have been shown in other experiments, such as when males skating in front of attractive researchers took more falls.

3. When attractive ladies are around, males contribute more money

According to research, the presence of hot men or women has no effect on a woman's monetary donating habits, while the presence of a hot woman motivates men to contribute more. According to this theory, a good deed is the human counterpart of the peacock's tail. In practice, this study demonstrates how cultures may foster altruistic behavior.

4. When males eat with women, they consume more calories

"Men don't want to be perceived as light eaters, whether unknowingly or intentionally, especially in front of women," according to a report from a 2011 research on college students' eating habits. Women consume less in front of men and more in front of other women, whereas men consume more in front of women. "The assumption is that when you're with the opposing gender, you're more conscious of gender and may desire to prove your gender more," said one of the study's co-authors. As a result, males should not be offended when women push them to finish their plates at restaurants, as this is simply a gender statement.

5. When males have to engage with women, their cognitive abilities are harmed

Men's cognitive function declines after engaging with attractive women, according to 2009 research. A more recent study found that merely thinking about connecting with ladies, or talking with ladies on the phone or in some other way when they can't see them, causes males to experience cognitive deterioration. Women, on the other hand, are not in the same boat.

6. The presence of women has an impact on how men handle their finances

The more women a man believes are around (to date him, for example), the more likely he is to save. When a man believes there are fewer women around, he is more inclined to overspend and get into debt. "We projected that fluctuations in sex ratio would be related with men's need for immediate gains," the research leader stated. "A male-biased sex ratio increases the degree to which males must compete for mates, and given the significance for men of displaying financial resources via spending and consumption, we predicted that shifts in sex ratio would be connected with men's desire for immediate gains."

7. Women have the ability to make their spouses talk more

Men are more talkative around their spouses, according to studies. Also, guys are often more chatty than women.

CHAPTER FOUR

What Do Real Men Want?

First and foremost, you must recognize that guys prefer basic things. They don't overthink every word you say in search of a hidden meaning, and they don't communicate in riddles. In fact, you may be confident that when a man says something, he means precisely what he says at the time. What exactly does this imply? It simply implies that men admire women who tell them how they feel and how they don't feel. Rather than implying that you are too tired to go out that evening or that you are dissatisfied that he isn't spending enough time with you, tell him. Yes, you risk being rejected, but you're also showing him what you want, and there's nothing a man loves more than not having to worry about upsetting you if he makes a mistake. Of course, delivery is crucial, and a guy will respond much more positively if you speak softly and femininely rather than yelling at him. Because guys desire to make their woman happy, being gentle and feminine utterly disarms him. If you start shouting, on the other hand, you're essentially competing with him, and he'll start treating you like one of the guys because men compete against one another. As a result, he'll either do the "man thing" or retreat within himself, or he'll try to compete with you. Men marry women who make them feel good, and since they have such a hard time accessing their own emotions, they enjoy being with women who do. Now, if he's always walking on eggshells because he doesn't know how to satisfy you, the last thing he'll feel good about himself is happiness.

Men Desire To Be Needed

Many women are afraid to acknowledge, even to themselves, that they want to be treasured and that they need a guy because of the way our society is built today. Even when they feel lonely without a spouse, admitting it is nearly heresy. Many women and you may be one of them, will tell you that they have a wonderful profession and date all the time but can't keep a relationship together. And they're baffled as to why. It's precisely because they've convinced themselves that they don't need a guy, and it's exactly what they project. Unfortunately, if a guy does not believe that a woman requires his assistance, he will believe that there is nothing he can do for her that she cannot accomplish on her own. He won't be able to play the role of knight in shining armor for his lady, and nothing makes a guy flee faster than the sensation that he isn't required. While independence might be beneficial in some aspects of life, it is often the most detrimental to relationships. Would you want to be with someone who claims they don't require your assistance? No one is implying that you should use him as an emotional crutch or give all authority to him, but you should be aware that the concept of equality in partnerships is greatly exaggerated. Indeed, if you were on an equal footing with him, you'd be treated like one of his buddies, and few women want to be treated like that. Guys, after all, never open out to each other, they're always competing on some level, and they don't embrace and kiss each other. Is that what you're looking for?

Men Tune Out When Women Use Too Much Words

When women are angry with their husbands, many believe that the best approach is to sit down and speak about it with him. She'll begin speaking at a breakneck speed, and a male will gradually tune her out. Then she'll become enraged because he isn't paying attention to her, and he won't understand why she is unhappy because "I can tell you everything you said." You must commit the following phrase to memory. MEN'S ATTENTION SPANS ARE SHORT, EVEN WHEN IT COMES TO PROBLEMS. Men have a funny habit of assuming that whatever problem you bring up is in some way his fault, even if you aren't attempting to blame him. Then he'll try to justify himself, which will enrage you even more, and things will devolve into a yelling fight. Because it is a type of competitiveness, guys do not respond to yelling or lecturing. Men, on the other hand, do react when they see the woman they love in agony, and they respond tenfold if they believe she isn't blaming them for her suffering. Men will go to great lengths to restore the grin on the face of the lady they adore. So, rather of embarking into a long explanation of what's bothering you, which will likely result in his tuning out soon after you begin, take a new approach. Simply express your feelings to him, but make it brief and sweet. You'll notice that he responds considerably more positively and is much more driven to remedy whatever it is that is bothering you. Another effective technique to attract his attention without competing with him is to just move away and maintain a safe distance. Yes, he will be alright at first, but he will soon begin to worry whether you are displeased with him, and he will come to you. He'll be more open if you don't have to push him to sit down and have "the discussion" with him.

Men Do Not Want To Compete With Their Female Counterparts.

Men do not wish to compete with their female partners. They don't marry for the sake of rivalry since they have plenty of it everywhere in their lives, from employment to friends. They want someone in whom they can confide, with whom they can have fun, and who will be devoted to them. Men desire peace and to satisfy their wives or girlfriends, so they try to avoid conflict in their relationships as much as possible. For a male, conflict equals to a competition, and men are built to do all in their power to win. Most guys will retreat because they do not want to lose their partner. As a result, if you adopt a different strategy and just refuse to debate, instead relying on your feelings to disarm him, you will discover that you are in charge. What did you do when you were a small girl and wanted to acquire something from your father? You exploited your emotions to make him feel like the finest parent on the earth, and you'd twirl him around your tiny finger no matter what mischief he got into. It was all for the sake of making his young child happy and putting a smile on her face because it made him happy. In relationships, the same is true, and if you can relearn how to use your feelings, you will discover that your boyfriend is lot more sensitive to you. He will want to do things for you just to make you happy, since that is what makes him happy. Nothing is more essential to a man than knowing that he can make his girlfriend happy.

Your Man's Empowerment

Women like attempting to alter guys. Let's face it, you know you do. How many times have you fell in love with the bad guy in a movie and secretly wished you could alter him? Consider the film American Psycho, which starred Christian Bale. Millions of women were swooning for a deranged killer with a chainsaw, not only because he was attractive, but because they believed they could alter him. In other words, they are more interested in his potential than in the guy he is now. That may be a worthwhile effort if you want to risk your life with someone like that, but if you try to apply the same strategy to your relationship, it will only serve to drive your boyfriend away. When men are trusted and appreciated for who they are, they feel empowered and cherished. In fact, a little gratitude might go a long way toward making him feel cherished. If you try to modify him, though, you are effectively telling him that he isn't good enough, competent enough, clever enough, and so on. As a consequence, even if you don't realize it, you'll be harming him. The more you attempt to alter him, the less he feels loved, trusted, and accepted by you. While women regard giving advice as a show of affection, males take it as a confirmation that they aren't trustworthy or worthy. Remember that men will only listen to advice if they ask for it. Instead of attempting to alter him by giving him unwanted advice, show your love by giving him your trust. You must fundamentally believe that he is capable of fixing his difficulties on his own. This isn't to say that you should keep your emotions hidden. It simply means you shouldn't use them as a kind of punishment or as a tool to influence him. You'll never be able to change him, and it'll just push the two of you away. If he's agitated, for example, you might be inclined to pry and poke him until he tells you what's upsetting him. However, he will see this as an attempt on your behalf to modify the way he handles his difficulties, leading him to believe you don't trust him. Instead, express some concern while mostly ignoring the fact that he is unhappy until he is ready to speak with you. Also, avoid giving him free advice since it will make him feel as though you don't accept him for who he is or that you don't trust him. Instead, be patient and trust that he will be able to mature on his own and will ultimately seek your counsel. Another common blunder women do is making sacrifices for their spouses without expecting anything in return. This, on the other hand, makes him feel as though you're attempting to influence his behavior. As a result, you should accomplish things for yourself rather than relying on him to make you happy. If you order him about, your guy will feel as if you are attempting to dominate him, just as you don't want him making decisions for you or telling you what to do. Relax and accept that life's flaws are what make it so lovely. What's more essential, after all? Is it more important that he cleaned beneath the table or his feelings?

On the Surface

While this may appear to be a little shallow, there is little we can do to change the reality that men are visual animals. This does not imply that you must see a plastic surgeon first thing in the morning to be transformed into Victoria's Secret runway model. Certain characteristics, on the other hand, make women far more appealing to males. Men, for example, are huge fans of long hair on women. It is a statement of femininity, and the only thing they enjoy more than long hair is seeing it tied back into a ponytail. The reason for this is that it has a minor sexual connotation because it accentuates your neck's delicate contours. Additionally, if you adopt a more feminine style by wearing dresses and skirts more frequently, you will attract more guys. This is due to the fact that in dresses, women seem softer and more feminine, and men are drawn to this like bees to honey. High heels are the last but not least. Heels do wonders for your posture and make guys fall head over heels in love with them. One argument is that wearing high heels causes you to walk more slowly and elegantly. In high heels, it's nearly difficult to move at rapid speed or with a lack of elegance. That is unless you want to shatter your neck. Also, while you're wearing heels, you know you feel fantastic on the inside. It boosts your self-esteem by making you feel taller and more appealing. You have a sense of being on top of the world. This self-assurance shines through, and guys notice it. Nothing attracts a man more than a woman who is confident and secure in her own skin.

CHAPTER FIVE

Be sexy

When it comes to sex, women's biggest difficulty is that they are extremely self-conscious. This causes you to lose concentration on what's going on, and you get so preoccupied with how you appear that you fail to enjoy what's going on. Not only that, but some women also express their fears, exacerbating the problem. Ladies, you must stop focusing on what you believe is wrong with you and instead embrace the present moment. If he's there with you and says you turn him on, believe him. Guys, after all, can't fake it. They can't possibly do it. He's already turned on by who you are right now if he's in the room with you. Pointing out your cellulite or attempting to conceal a region of your body for fear of seeming big or unsteady is like throwing a spotlight on it for him to see when he would probably never have seen otherwise. Men simply don't see the flaws we consider flaws unless you bring them out. Another issue that many couples face is that sex becomes ordinary and then gradually dries up and ceases. We, as well as society, share responsibility for this. We forget that sex should be enjoyable as well as a wonderful opportunity to bond with your spouse. A story was told of a couple in their nineties who had been married for almost sixty years. However, they were still profoundly in love with each other, as seen by their physical expressions of affection. Tony recommended they go to their room because they were having so much fun. When asked what their secret was, the pair said they would try everything once, among other things. They would do it again if they like it. To put it another way, variety is the spice of life, and sex isn't anything to be embarrassed about. The more diversity you have in your sex life, the less likely it is to become monotonous and a chore rather than a pleasure You may keep your sex relationship interesting by surprise your lover with an unexpected frolicking or role playing for him, and you can be as creative as you like sure he'll want to join in. Keep in mind that the ideal romantic evening does not have to be a Movie production. A hot, sweaty, quick roll in the hay is sometimes just what the doctor prescribed. You'll also learn that it's an excellent way to unwind. However, don't expect to have a great conversation with him and then be disappointed when he falls asleep. Men find it difficult to express their emotions at any time, let alone after a good night's sex when their brain has fully shut down.

CHAPTER SIX

How to Be the Woman Every Man Desires

Men regard some women as "marriage material" and others not so much, no matter how much we disagree with this. So you'll wonder, "What's the difference?" Here's how to be the woman every man wants to marry in order to keep him dedicated and show him that you're the only one for him.

1. Make a point of doing nice things for him. Men are typically expected to do all of the legwork in terms of scheduling dates and procuring presents. A guy would enjoy it if you pamper him, offer him sincere praises, and show him how much you value him.

2. Appearances do important, so dress the part. You don't always have to appear picture-perfect; we all have terrible hair days, but guys appreciate it when you're well-dressed and stunning.

3. Demonstrate how much you believe in him and how much you support him. It matters a lot to a man when his woman believes in him and his talents instead of dismissing or condemning him.

4. Avoid being clingy. Even after marriage, a couple can thrive if they maintain their own lifestyles. Men enjoy it when you give them their space since it indicates that you care about them.

5. Be there for him even if he doesn't want to chat. Even when they are anxious, most guys do not discuss their difficulties. A guy will feel supported and cared for simply by being at his side and present.

6. Men enjoy paying for you and bringing you out, but they respect a woman who can get

by on her own and occasionally offers to pay. It demonstrates to him that you are self-sufficient, capable of managing your finances (spending wisely), and are not reliant on him.

7. For a change, do something he enjoys doing. We know you generally bring him to watch a girl film and take him to your favorite places but try to do something he enjoys for a change. Watch a football game, play video games, or go bowling with him.

8. Plan ahead of time and don't be afraid to broach the subject of the future, but leave space for spontaneity. Don't set any limitations on your relationship or start talking about marriage too soon. That irritates a man.

9. Have faith in yourself. When you don't love yourself, how can you expect others to love you? Do not concentrate on your insecurities before letting them go. A man will always adore you just as you are.

10. Look after him. Bring him lunch on a hectic day when he hasn't eaten anything. Make his favorite dessert for him. Stuff like this demonstrates to a man that he can rely on you to help him feel better after a tough day.

11. Ask for his assistance and opinion on crucial matters. Yes, an independent woman is appealing, but men need to feel needed. Nonetheless, avoid appearing powerless and desperate; it's unpleasant.

12. Learn about his family and friends. Even if he doesn't realize it, a man will regard you differently if you get along with his family. If you also received his friends' approval, that's a double whammy!

13. When you're incorrect, admit it and apologize. Nobody likes those who never acknowledge they're wrong because they believe they're better than everyone else. Allow yourself to swallow your pride and apologize when required.

14. Express your gratitude and show him how much you appreciate what he does for you. Nothing makes a man happier than knowing they've done something special for you.

15. Be adaptable, relaxed, and spontaneous, but not irresponsible. Men are drawn to women who recognize their own value and do not seek external validation. They want a lady who is comfortable and not seeking attention.

16. Avoid unneeded drama. Drama queens become mad cat women. Please accept my apologies. If you indulge in drama on a daily basis, no healthy man will want to be your spouse. It's harsh, but it's true.

17. Let him know and comprehend you on a deeper level by opening your heart to him. A man does not want to marry a lady he has never met.

18. Don't keep your genuine objectives hidden. If you want to marry or focus on your

work for a few years, be honest about it from the start.

19. Always strive to improve yourself and your relationship. You convey to them how indifferent you are if you neglect to work on yourself. You set a positive example for your relationship's future growth by exhibiting constant progress.

20. Be merciful. Men usually misunderstand us and what we desire, and as a result, they make several errors. We're not suggesting you should immediately suppress your sentiments and forgive him, but you shouldn't hold it against him every time you quarrel.

CONCLUSION

If you want to be the woman who all men admire, you must first understand them. The more you know about a man and how he thinks and acts, the more likely you are to be able to personify his ideal woman. This isn't to say you should build a character that isn't true to yourself. Unfortunately, many women are scared to exhibit their actual selves because they believe it would make them appear weak. The trouble is that the more you hide your genuine self, the more resentment you build up inside, whether you know it or not since you are putting up a front that has nothing to do with who you truly are. If you learn to love and accept yourself, you will exude the confidence that guys find alluring. And by admitting to yourself that you need a guy in your life, you will suddenly feel free and more open. You won't put on the harsh front of "I don't need anybody," which turns off most guys, since, as we've seen, men like to be wanted. A guy wants to take care of a woman, to be her hero, and a woman who is entirely self-sufficient and exudes fierce independence will turn men off. Of sure, some men want strong women who take the lead, but most women, regardless of how strong or independent they are, do not want to be the ones to defend them. Even if she refuses to accept it to herself at first. The difficulty is that if you are dishonest with yourself, you may engage in a relationship that may harm both of you. The reason for this is that you initially project one thing before opening up and revealing your weakness and need for assistance. He will then feel cheated since you are a different person, resulting in animosity on both sides and a tragic ending. As a result, simply embrace who you are and allow yourself to be a woman. In fact, be proud of your femininity and remember that men want to make their ladies happy because it makes them feel wonderful. All men admire a woman who isn't afraid to exhibit her softer side, to demonstrate how much she needs her guy, and to recognize the basic distinctions between men and women. She will be able to respond to him better and establish a tranquil, loving family if she understands how he reacts differently. Nothing is more appealing to a man than a woman who has enough faith in him to be vulnerable with him. He will go to great lengths to satisfy you and make you smile since men melt when they see the woman they love to smile.

When they see the lady they love smiling at him, they feel free to be vulnerable with him. He will move mountains to please you and make you happy, because guys are wonderful.

www.ingramcontent.com/pod-product-compliance
Lightning Source LLC
LaVergne TN
LVHW052059160826
845678LV00015B/3298

* 9 7 9 8 4 2 0 8 4 0 2 5 2 *